Popular Individualism

An Introduction to the
No Turning Back Group, 1985-90

By Dr Tim Aker

© Tim Aker

Published in 2025 by The Bruges Group

ISBN: 978-1-917743-14-3

The Bruges Group Publications Office
246 Linen Hall, 162-168 Regent Street, London W1B 5TB
www.brugesgroup.com

Bruges Group publications are not intended to represent a corporate view of European and international developments. Contributions are chosen on the basis of their intellectual rigour, and their ability to open up new avenues for debate.

Twitter @brugesgroup, LinkedIn @brugesgroup
GETTR @brugesgroup, Telegram t.me/brugesgroup, Facebook @brugesgroup
Instagram @brugesgroup, YouTube @brugesgroup

SCAN FOR MORE BOOKS

By the Same Author

The First Brexiteer
The Diaries of Sir Neil Marten, 1970 – 79

Contents

Author's Note	1
Introduction	3
Part I	6
Part II	9
Part III	13
Part IV	18
Part V	25
Part VI	31
Part VII	36
About the Author	37
About the Bruges Group	38

Author's Note

Political history is dominated by the 'turning point', an event or series of incidents that send public affairs down one of two forks in the road. This primer explains one important to contemporary British political history: the birth of the No Turning Back group (NTB) in 1985 and the sizeable impact its ideas had on Mrs Thatcher, her administration and the narrative behind, what we know as, Thatcherism.

I want to thank Sir Gerald Howarth for access to his private papers, without which my doctoral thesis, and this primer, would not have been possible. I am also grateful to the Bruges Group for publishing this booklet and the Institute of Economic Affairs for hosting its launch. It is a tribute to the Institute's lasting influence in British politics. That the IEA acted as the incubator for the NTB reflected its mission to change politics through ideas. For a full account of the excellent work of the IEA, do read Richard Cockett's *Thinking the Unthinkable: Think-Tanks and the Economic Counter-Revolution, 1931-83*. This research is more succinct and focuses on how the Thatcherites looked beyond narrow monetarism and sought to make individualism genuinely popular. The NTB gave Thatcherism a stronger, bolder narrative.

Governments that do not have a narrative end up losing the very people they were elected to represent. Narratives give voters hope, even when tough and difficult decisions must be made. For the NTB that narrative was individual liberty, hence the title of this book. They ensured their arguments were designed to win a majority for individualism. In true Thatcherite style, it was to be a permanent revolution in stages.

History doesn't repeat, it rhymes. Even though some of these ideas and debates are forty-years old, there is plenty in here to give today's policy makers pause for thought. The state is too big, our economy too weak, authoritarianism too visible and our future too bleak. If any party seeking government can take inspiration from the NTB to fix these recurring ills, then we as a nation will benefit greatly.

Tim Aker
Kent, September 2025.

Introduction

In 1985 Arthur Seldon of the Institute of Economic Affairs (IEA) brought together a band of bright young New Rightists to examine Thatcherism and ask, 'what next?'. Public spending continued to creep up and, to these eager idealistic Thatcherites, the revolution had barely begun. They criticised the 'socialism' of the Old Right and wanted more freedom. Markets meant morality and were the means of an ordered society. Very few even considered themselves conservatives. They yearned for the transformational heat of Gladstonian liberalism. Seldon wrote that the Conservative party should take note, or the Social Democrats could offer these classical liberal Thatcherites a new home if, and it was a big if, the SDP abandoned its 'collectivist tendencies'.[1]

Seldon's anthology was timely. In 1985 the old ideological wounds within the Conservative party were once again torn open. The monetarist experiment, abolition of exchange controls, the 1981 budget, the Falklands War, and the beginning of trade union reform were all radical policies that set Mrs Thatcher apart from her predecessors in her first term. Yet after the 1983 election and a great 144-seat majority, the government appeared hesitant about what to do next.

Despite victory in the miners' strike and the roll out of privatisation, the second Thatcher term was riddled with concern that the government was not going far enough in tackling the growth of public expenditure. As early as July 1983 there was a 'lack of direction' and although Mrs Thatcher had a vision for Britain, there was

---

[1] Arthur Seldon, 'The Spectre that haunts the Left', in Arthur Seldon eds., *The New Right Enlightenment: Young Writers on the Spectre haunting the Left* (Sevenoaks: Economic and Literary Books, 1985), p. xi.

'no programme for achieving it'.[2] Observers noted that she now looked tired, her famous four hours of sleep a night and the strains and pressures of the first term had taken a noticeable toll on her energy. Some have even suggested the government stumbled into privatising nationalised industries 'by accident, driven more by Treasury cost-cutting than ideological conviction'.[3] Indeed, for all the reforms that were to follow, state spending continued to climb because Mrs Thatcher would not tackle spending on social programmes.[4]

Out of this concern a group of Conservative MPs formed the 'No Turning Back' group in November 1985. It marked a turning point in Conservative politics. Rather than factionalising into conspiratorial ginger groups as Labour MPs were prone, Conservatives traditionally banded together in dining clubs. These evolved from social gatherings, designed to make late-night parliamentary debates tolerable, into a means of political organisation. They operated on both left and right of the party. Its most popular 'right' (or Thatcherite) organisation was the 92 Group, named after the Chelsea townhouse in Cheyne Walk of its first chairman, Sir Patrick Wall. On the left were the Lollards, so named after Lollards Tower that was the London home of its convenor Sir William van Straubenzee, the Crown Estates Commissioner. Also on the left was Nick's Diner, named after Tory MP Nicholas Scott. By the mid-80s the 92 had routed these groups from the backbench policy committees, which at the time was the barometer of party opinion.

---

[2] Charles Moore, *Margaret Thatcher: The Authorized Biography: Volume Two* (London: Penguin, 2016), p. 80.
[3] John Campbell, *Margaret Thatcher: Volume Two* (London: Jonathan Cape, 2003), p. 94.
[4] Ibid., p. 82.

The NTB were different and broke with the tradition of meddling in backbench committee elections. Their battlefield was ideas. The 92 Group made sure that Thatcherites were in control of the significant backbench committees. But the 92 didn't publish papers, its focus was on mobilisation and campaigning, a tactic driven by its chairman Sir George Gardiner. By contrast the NTB was complementary to the 92: they published sophisticated pamphlets, and its members achieved high government office, and some members of the NTB were also members of the 92. Their ideas became deeply influential and shaped government policy after 1985.

The NTB were sorely needed. Paradoxically, the safer Mrs Thatcher was in terms of a parliamentary majority, especially after her landslide victory in 1983, the more those on her own side began to question where the ship was headed. This is what spurred the NTB into action and, at its fortieth anniversary this year, this primer will examine its foundations and its papers from 1985-90 and argue that they inspired the political development of late-term Thatcherism and successor governments – Conservative *and* Labour.

I

Mrs Thatcher's administration was noted for its caution. This, however, cannot be confused with timidity. She was careful but ready to go 'all-in' when the time was right. It explains her tactical retreats, most notably a U-turn on mine closures in 1981 that horrified her loyalist backbenchers. Yet the lessons of that episode set in place a plan to hoard coal for an inevitable showdown with the soon-to-be President of the National Union of Mineworkers (NUM), Arthur Scargill, in 1984.

The monetarist experiment of 1979-81 was, however, a sign that there would be no retreat from substantially reforming the post-war consensus. It had been an almighty task few believed the Prime Minister was prepared for or would see through. For the first woman Prime Minister, who had only been Education Secretary, to take on the masculine might of the trade unions so soon after they had been seen to bring down two administrations in the 1970s, was itself a very brave thing to attempt. To do so at the same time as she ushered in an ideologically monetarist policy to combat inflation through control of the money supply was, in hindsight, remarkable.

Yet by 1981 it had not seen a concomitant reduction in the size and role of the state, if judged in terms of the amount spent by the government. Spotting an opportunity, Lord Ralph Harris of High Cross, the director of the IEA ennobled by Mrs Thatcher in 1979, formed a Repeal Group in the House of Lords. Its aim was to nominate laws for abolition to cut back the frontiers of the state. Originally it aimed at low hanging fruit, such as government controls on the sale of spectacles.

After the 1983 election a group of Thatcherite MPs were invited to the Lords Repeal Group as observers. All, bar Michael Brown, had been elected in the 1983 landslide. Taking inspiration and a prompt from Lord Harris, they then formed their own Commons version that sought to not only repeal anachronistic legislation, but to change the terms of debate on public services in the UK. They dined regularly at the IEA, and it was as if the IEA now had a political wing in the Conservative party: a group determined to put into action policies that rolled back the frontiers of the state.

On 22 November 1983 the first meeting of the unnamed Commons 'repeal' group met.[5] It followed in the steps of the Lords Repeal group by seeking to do away with out-of-date legislation. It also agreed to campaign for 'reform of the NHS in the direction of charges and insurance'. This was extremely controversial. In 1982 the government's 'think tank', the Central Policy Review Staff (CPRS), had sealed its fate by recommending that the government introduce charges in the National Health Service. Mrs Thatcher was horrified, but more out of caution than ideological disgust. As punishment the CPRS was abolished in 1983.

The Commons Repeal group eventually named themselves 'The Disciples', not specifying whether of Hayek, Friedman or Adam Smith. Recognising that the party was at risk of drifting, they opted to take on the consolidators within the party. Whereas the Lords Repeal Group focused on 'specific issues', the Disciples would 'provide a commentary on all aspects of economic and social policy'. By doing so they would act as 'a

---

[5] The twelve MPs were Michael Brown, Peter Bruinvels, Michael Fallon, Michael Forsyth, Alan Howarth, Gerald Howarth, Robert Jones, Francis Maude, Richard Ryder. Invited but not attending were Christopher Chope, Peter Lilley, and Neil Hamilton.

strong counterweight to those they think are pushing Prime Minister Margaret Thatcher towards the centre'. Publicity had its downside for the Disciples, however, as 'strong regrets' were raised at the group's name, and they agreed to change it in due course.[6]

What the 'Disciples' got right, however, was that the government was in trouble. Reports in early 1984 lamented the government's detachment from its backbenches, clearly missing the essential role played by Ian Gow who had been a senior member of the 92 and Mrs Thatcher's parliamentary private secretary (PPS) in her first term.[7] Lord Harris highlighted two editorials in *The Times* shortly after the launch that were critical of the government for not going further in its reform programme. The first, dated 23 March, decried the government's 'lack of progress' in reducing 'the role of the state in people's lives'. Granted, it had brought down inflation in the first parliament, but this was 'because the reduction in inflation was a paramount objective to which all else was subordinated'. *The Times* concluded that the same revolutionary zeal was not directed to 'the Government's commitment to get the state off people's backs'. The same paper the next day attacked the Prime Minister's caution. It laid out a series of cuts that could be made in a retort to the Prime Minister's comments that 'it is not possible to cut public expenditure below the plans we indicated' at the election.[8]

---

[6] Howarth papers, Lord Harris to 'Disciples', 28 March 1984.
[7] THCR 2/6/3/16/part2/ f53, Peter Riddell, 'Tories increasingly critical of Thatcher's inner circle', *Financial Times*, 21 February 1984.
[8] Howarth papers, Lord Harris to 'Disciples', 28 March 1984.

II

The drift was an open opportunity for Mrs Thatcher's internal opposition who, whilst defeated, had lain dormant. In 1984 Francis Pym rejoined the battle. In 1980 he had developed a support base across the party after he successfully shielded the defence budget from cuts. The right-wing backbencher Alan Clark had told him that should he resign, in defence of his departmental budget, he could count on support across the party and would end up as Prime Minister within two years. Instead, Pym and party chairman Lord Thorneycroft conducted a clandestine campaign within the administration to undermine government policy, which might have worked had the 92 Group not been there to rebuff the rebel attacks.

In 1982 Pym became Foreign Secretary during the Falklands conflict, a promotion that was a nod to his wartime experience rather than any strong bond of loyalty between Pym and the Prime Minister. At the height of the conflict, he attempted to strongarm the war cabinet into agreeing a peace deal based on an American plan that amounted to joint sovereignty of the Islands with the Argentines. Mrs Thatcher was aghast and acknowledged that if his plan went through, she could not stay as Prime Minister. In the war cabinet John Nott crucially recommended that the deal be put to the Argentines first before the government made a decision.[9] That they did not accept it scuppered Pym's plan for a negotiated peace.

Although Pym was kept on as Foreign Secretary after the conflict, he signed his own political death

---

[9] Dominic Sandbrook, *Who Dares Wins: Britain, 1979-1982* (London: Penguin, 2019), p. 784.

warrant during the 1983 election. During the campaign on BBC *Question Time*, Pym said that landslides did not produce successful governments. His punishment duly came after the election. Mrs Thatcher tried to convince him to become Speaker, but he instead retreated to the backbenches where her judgement was that he was not a very effective critic of the government.[10]

Mrs Thatcher's assessment was correct. In 1984 Pym published *The Politics of Consent*. It was a forthright but not original critique of government policy, leadership, and philosophy. He focused on unemployment, which was still over three million in 1985, and the weak spot of the government. The economy had been liberalised and was returning to growth, but success was marred with so many people out of work. Pym advocated spending on public works, specifically housing, communications and public utilities. There should be more regional policy, planning and intervention, all of which had been tried before. Revenues from privatisation should be directed to this end. He suggested an extra £4bn, an amount not dissimilar to that spent combating the miners' strike.[11] It was back to consensus politics in ends and means. Mrs Thatcher, he said, was too confrontational, too single minded, too ideological. She didn't care about the unemployed. It was all the usual tropes from a politician who had missed his chance.

On 12 May 1985 a vehicle for Pym's politics, Centre Forward, was launched amidst much media

---

[10] Margaret Thatcher, *The Downing Street Years* (London: HarperCollins, 1993), pp. 306-7.
[11] Francis Pym, *The Politics of Consent* (London: Sphere Books Ltd., 1985), pp. 9-13,

fanfare.¹² Although the threat only lasted a week, it was a dire warning. Pym claimed the group, which he boasted was thirty-strong, was there to change Conservative policy but not its leader. This had been the same line the party's 'wets' had used in the early 1980s. Within days it fell apart. As a *Times* editorial noted, Pym was critical of government economic policy, yet the United Kingdom was 'the only country apart from the United States to have regained its earlier growth rates' after the global recession of the early 1980s.¹³

Pym, clearly, should have known better, especially as a former Chief Whip. In surrounding himself with the likes of Ian Gilmour, Geoffrey Rippon, and Julian Critchley, he united under his banner the same discredited Heathites who had sought to dislodge Mrs Thatcher in 1980-1. Centre Forward split between those who wanted to challenge Mrs Thatcher and those who didn't want to rock the boat. It never recovered. In the two years after the launch of Centre Forward, Pym had gone from being Mrs Thatcher's chief critic and most prominent challenger to being out of parliament – he stood down in 1987.

Centre Forward, though, was a warning to the Thatcherites. Whilst Thatcherism had returned the country to economic growth, unemployment was still painfully high. The government had broken with orthodoxy and upturned the post-war consensus within its first term. It had defeated the trades unions, when in the past it had been the unions that defeated governments. But by November 1985 spending had increased markedly from the halcyon days of revolution in 1979-80, when the government had desperately tried

---

[12] Stephen Evans, 'A Tiny Little Footnote in History': Conservative Centre Forward', *Parliamentary History*, 29 (2010), 208-228, (p. 208).
[13] Leader, 'Centre Backward', *The Times*, 15 May 1985, p. 15.

to control the growth of expenditure. The social security budget had increased by twenty-eight per cent, health by sixteen per cent and industry by nearly eighteen per cent.[14] That November the government considered a freeze on public spending as a victory. This was a far cry from the £5bn of cuts Mrs Thatcher had demanded in July 1981. Something had to be done to bring Thatcherism back on track.

---

[14] Martin Holmes, *Thatcherism: Scope and Limits, 1983-87* (London: Palgrave, 1989), p. 27.

III

The Disciples asked to meet Mrs Thatcher on 18 June 1985 for an historic discussion that prompted their first pamphlet. Timing here is key; this meeting was only a few weeks after Centre Forward launched. The meeting was a success, and the pamphlet *No Turning Back* 'in part [...] sprang' from the meeting they had with Mrs Thatcher.[15]

On 3 November 1985 the group published *No Turning Back: A New Agenda from a Group of Conservative MPs*, which gave the group its final name. It combined policy proposals of a think tank paper with the propaganda value of a political communication. It began with an analysis of the modern state which applied constraints on individuals and enterprise, concentrated power in the hands of the bureaucracy, and implemented standardisation of production, even 'substantardisation'. Since 1979 the decline of the United Kingdom had been reversed and the old ways of consensus had broken down. The changes recommended by the NTB, however radical, were only the start. Choice and opportunity had to be opened up and widened further through the 'free choices of individuals'.

Market forces provided the means, through choice, to maximise individual freedom. Individuals expressed 'their preferences by their actions'. Diversity within the market gave the consumer 'sovereignty' to 'decide more of their own lives by their choices'. The overriding goal was to rescue the free market from the monetarist experiment so associated with recession and high unemployment. Their mission was to show that the

---

[15] THCR2/1/4/40 f25, Stephen Sherbourne to Margaret Thatcher, 3 November 1985.

free economy was more than an abstraction 'cooked up by a few monetarists in finance houses'. It needed to be practical and broad in its application. It also had to be seen to be majoritarian, a mass transfer of power through market mechanisms. It had some surprising proposals on education, health, housing, and unemployment.

On education the NTB recommended three measures to widen choice and combat the politicisation of education. The first was to give schools more autonomy and control of their curriculum and staff. School boards were to be elected by a postal vote franchise. The headteacher would be appointed by the board, be accountable to it, and would run the school as a *de facto* chief executive. Second, funding should follow the child. The NTB critique of 1980s education, and much of the public sector, was that funding was allocated to satisfy the producer and not the consumer. Therefore, this naturally led to the third prong of the programme. With funding following the pupils state schools could expand with demand. Bad schools would lose pupils, but it would be a sign for their board to make improvements. Ultimately, it was a programme for quality and not 'equality'.

Some of these proposals were ahead of their time. The NTB encouraged the uptake of student loans and the phasing out of grants for university education. It was a very radical concept. Student loans had been rejected by Mrs Thatcher previously when the CPRS mooted them in 1982.[16] They were finally introduced under Tony Blair in his New Labour administration: such was the influence the NTB had on its political opponents as well as on the Conservative party.

---

[16] Howarth papers, Peter Riddell, 'Tory group in "stay radical" plea', *Financial Times*, 2 November 1985.

Its offering on 'unemployment' was to first recognise that the improvement in the economic situation had not resulted in a cut in unemployment, which in 1985 was still over three million. Indeed, 'a jobless boom' was 'too cold a thing to excite popular support'. There needed to be a two-pronged approach to create the conditions for employment in the private sector and defeat the poverty trap to make sure it always benefitted a person to work rather than claim state handouts. They recommended liberal reforms, such as allowing those on the payroll to change their status to self-employed to reduce business costs and allow flexibility in the workplace. Unsurprisingly they advocated cuts in capital taxes, taking inspiration from the Kennedy administration of the early 1960s that had reduced rates but brought in more revenue. They also called for lower income taxes to make sure work paid, a consistent Thatcherite policy advocated as far back as the 1979 budget. Yet for the NTB it was not about shifting from direct to indirect taxation, the overall burden had to be cut. 'Several' per cent had to come off income and corporate taxes as well as significant widening of the bands to make sure enterprise was not discouraged.

Whereas Francis Pym's *Politics of Consent* advocated the revenues from asset sales be 'reinvested' into public works, the NTB insisted that the government use the revenue to endow tax cuts which would sustain dynamic economic activity for the longer term. If the government extended its privatisation programme it could knock six pence off the basic rate. It would herald a virtuous spiral of the state retreating and enterprise, personal freedom, and choice advancing. To supplement this, they called on the government to deregulate. Examples included exempting small businesses from health and safety legislation. Small firms were the 'vanguard' of job creation. They required special status where firms of fewer than twenty staff should be exempt from swathes of regulations and immune from penalties. They looked to the Italian example where a similar scheme had worked. These would, they argued, lead to a change in mindsets. Whereas in the 1960s and 1970s wealth and profit were 'frowned upon', to resolve the unemployment crisis attitudes had to change.

Health, as much then as it has always been, was a more delicate area for the NTB and they approached it with nuance. They maintained that the security the NHS gave to patients had to be preserved. No one could live with the fear that if they couldn't afford healthcare, they wouldn't receive it. Much like their approach to education, they analysed the problem from the view of the consumer rather than the producer. Under the existing NHS model there was no way for consumer preferences to be taken into account. The state model was monopolistic and, inevitably, rationed with spending dictated by political criteria.

Since 1979 private healthcare had increased: out of the £17bn spent on healthcare, £1bn was spent in the private sector. The government had already encouraged private use by making premiums tax deductible for those earning under £8,500 as an enrolled employee (around £32,000 in today's prices). The NTB wanted to increase the threshold and extend it to the self-employed. This way they could widen choice to those in work and make private use more affordable. Other policies aimed to transfer funding to the clinical side of the NHS, contracting out cleaning, and by introducing management from the private sector into the management of hospitals. Of all the areas covered in their first pamphlet, it is the thinnest, but they would return to the theme in a later paper.

Finally, they examined housing, one of the 'biggest success stories' of the Thatcher administration. The right to buy had seen a massive shift in property, a transfer of state assets to private ownership that had been a long time coming. Indeed, it had featured in the early discussion documents of the 92 Group in the 1960s. It was, however, only a start. The NTB wanted to liberalise as much of the housing market as possible, including the repeal of rent controls and unlimited security of tenure for new rents. Rents should also go towards the purchase of property, giving renters the goal of ownership. Above all they encouraged policies to widen property ownership as much as possible, even encouraging the transfer of dilapidated blocks and properties from the state to the private sector for renovation and then sale or rent. It sought to continue the transfer of power and assets from the state sector into individual and private hands.

In conclusion, this revolutionary pamphlet sought to advance Thatcherism into its next stage. It was a determination to defend the 'spontaneity of society' through which individuals could make choices over the allocation of resources as an expression of their preferences and priorities. Rather than the state making decisions, the scales should be tipped towards individuals at the micro level. A leader in the *Daily Telegraph* commended their proposals for being 'popular as well as right'.[17]

---

[17] Howarth papers, Leader, 'No Backsliding', *Daily Telegraph*, 4 November 1985.

IV

The NTB followed *No Turning Back* with pamphlets on education in 1986 and health in 1988. They spurred two significant pieces of legislation reforming the delivery of these essential services. The first of the two, *Save Our Schools*, sought to build on the proposals in *No Turning Back* and, crucially, deal with the voucher question. Consistent throughout the NTB's papers was its focus on consumer choice. Choice enabled individuals to express their preferences, which in turn revealed knowledge on what was working and what was not. Their critique of the public sector was that the system, rather than being based on the interests of the consumer, was entirely based on the needs of the producer. To the NTB this meant more spending, higher taxes, and more state controls. Inevitably this introduced politics into public services leading, as they wrote, to the teaching of peace studies and anti-racism instead of core subjects.

Students of Conservative politics would look at their analysis and immediately expect the NTB to laud grammar schools and private education. Surprisingly, they did not. Grammar schools, they argued, provided for so few that they could not be a general solution to the education question. They were only a choice in the mix. The NTB were more ambitious and wanted fundamental change so that all parents could exercise individual choice. To them individualism could only be achieved if it was ably exercised by the greatest number of individuals. The comprehensives had destroyed choice and technical education. Just as top-down economic planning had been a disaster, the same was true of education. Metrics were based on the needs of the producer. For instance, the NTB gave the example of

Japanese education where students outperformed British pupils in classes twice as large.[18]

Free market solutions to education inevitably return to the question of vouchers. In theory parents could take the pound value of a state education to any school, public or state, and top up with their own resources if required, supported with tax rebates. It would be a free market in education by radically extending choice for parents. In practice, however, the NTB found that this would only partially extend choice. The independent sector was not big enough for the voucher system to work. At 1985/6 levels only seven per cent of students were in private education. Assuming a voucher scheme led to 'unprecedented' uptake in private education, and it increased by three times, it would still leave three quarters of students in the state sector.[19] As they wrote, in theory it was admirable but there were serious political flaws. Whilst ideal for a new society, practical measures were needed. They wanted everyone to get a taste of individual freedom and choice which, later, would lead to the irreversible liberalisation of the education sector. This was Mrs Thatcher's view in 1983 when vouchers were discussed. The priority, she said, should be to widen choice 'in the maintained sector'. Action in the 'independent sector' may follow at a later stage.[20]

Save our Schools expanded upon the themes of *No Turning Back*. Their solution was operational independence for all schools funded by the state. Each school should be run by an elected school board. The board would appoint a headteacher as CEO on a five-year contract. Schools would be structured as

---

[18] No Turning Back Group, *Save Our Schools* (London: CPC, 1986), p. 10.
[19] Ibid., pp. 12-3.
[20] PREM19/1011 f35, No. 10 record of conversation, 29 March 1983.

'independent, autonomous units'.[21] To provide choice within the state sector, funding would follow the pupil. Consequently, school funding would relate to the number of students enrolled via direct grants and spent by the board/CEO. Schools would have the freedom to tap new resources of finance and freedom to set the school day, curriculum, and even religious denomination. Schools would set their own acceptance criteria, standards and emphasis.

This funding mechanism would also permit schools to expand to meet demand. Each school would be an experimental centre, and each would learn from the other to get the best outcomes. Popular schools would expand, underperforming schools would either adapt or close. In structure and operation, it would be the complete opposite to the comprehensives but operating *within* the state sector. The only input from the state would be the funding. Like a voucher, choice would be given to the parents to which state school they sent their children. Unlike the voucher system, capacity would be there for immediate use and without the need to top up with fees. Power to decide the education and operation of the school would transfer from the state to the parents. This level of choice, as opposed to the immediate implementation of a voucher system, would be 'irreversible'.[22]

Save Our Schools was their most successful paper. Its influence can be seen in the Education Act 1988 and the policies of successive Conservative and *Labour* administrations. Taking heed right from its pages, the Thatcher administration created 'Grant Maintained' school status in the Education Act 1988. Governing

---

[21] NTB, *Save Our Schools*, p. 17.
[22] Ibid., p. 22.

bodies became the 'boards' and took over responsibility for school property, staffing, pay, and admissions policy.[23] Parents and communities could ballot for the creation of Grant Maintained status and, if successful, they became independent of local authority control on the agreement of the Secretary of State. As the NTB wrote, it was an irreversible direction of travel.

Although the Blair administration abolished Grant Maintained status in 1998, they replaced them with Foundation Schools, a watered-down version but one that still gave governing bodies powers over hiring, property use and maintenance. Two years later, Blair displayed impeccable Thatcherite credentials with the creation of Academy Schools. Academies are state financed but independent of local authority control. They were given powers to pay bonuses and introduce business management and financial sponsorship, through trusts, into education – something recommended in *Save Our Schools*.[24] A further innovation from the 2010 Coalition government was Free Schools, a type of Academy that had more flexibility on what it taught and whether it could specialise. It was a further extension of parental choice. Free Schools could be run by universities, charities, businesses or religious organisations. Again, it was right from the pages of *Save Our Schools*.

In 1988, off the success of *Save Our Schools*, the NTB produced *The NHS: A Suitable Case for Treatment*. It sought to apply the same principles of the education pamphlet to the NHS, specifically that choice be widened within the state sector. This, however, was more problematic. Buoyed from what it saw as its successful

---

[23] Howarth papers, Charles Hymas, 'Right turn ahead?', *Yorkshire Post*, 18 September 1990.
[24] NTB, *Save Our Schools*, pp. 19-20.

role in shaping the 1988 Education Act, it called on the government not to wait until its fourth term to challenge the problems within the NHS.[25] The NHS, like education, had the same issues in that the service was viewed from the producer interest instead of the consumer. The NHS budget had increased by forty per cent since 1979, even accounting for inflation, and yet there were still problems with waiting lists and accusations of underfunding. As they diagnosed, 'when a service is free at the point of consumption, the demand for it is literally infinite'. Therefore, service providers had no incentive to allocate resources efficiently. Worse, under a state system rationing is inevitable and evolved into, as the NTB put it, 'hostage medicine' as the problems within the NHS became politicised.[26]

The NTB prescription was for hospitals to become independent within the state sector. This meant opening the NHS to private management, turning them into individual trusts, and allowing hospitals to specialise to widen patient choice. Further to this there should be better coordination and cooperation with the private sector. The NHS should be allowed to purchase services from the private sector. They pointed to existing tendering for ancillary services which had saved, at 1988 prices, £100m for the NHS already.[27] The management of hospitals should be made up of boards and governors, like their proposals for schools. The decentralisation of management would increase efficiency and resource allocation missing from the mindset of a service free at the point of use.

---

[25] NTB, *The NHS: A Suitable Case for Treatment* (London: CPC, 1988), p. 5.
[26] Ibid., pp. 6-7. The 'war of Jennifer's ear' in the 1992 election campaign serves as a case in point when the treatment of a child's ear infection became a national news story.
[27] Ibid., p. 23.

As with vouchers, the NTB addressed a funding model based purely on insurance as a free-market, shock-therapy alternative to the NHS. Whilst appealing in theory, its downside was an inevitable price spiral of soaring premiums. Instead, NHS spending should follow the patient in a reformed system of independently managed hospitals along the board structure not too different from those proposed for schools. Therefore, health services should be commissioned from 'a per-capita budget by specialised management teams'. Patients would therefore have optimum choice available within the NHS for GP services, hospital services, and other care.

Again, the government listened. In 1989 they published a White Paper entitled *Working for Patients*. The paper outlined plans to give patients choice within the NHS. Hospitals were allowed to be self-governing as NHS Trusts and earn revenue from services they provided. This, like the schools policy, enabled funding to follow the patient, thus rewarding good hospitals and forcing underperforming ones to adapt and change. These reforms grew into the 'Internal Market' of the NHS and in the National Health Service and Community Care Act 1990, given royal assent months before Mrs Thatcher left office. In the Act the government established NHS Trusts which owned and managed hospitals, giving them the freedom to borrow, generate income, raise money from other sources and, crucially, decide who to purchase care from. The parallels with *Save Our Schools* are stark and were as irreversible as the education reforms. Again, the hero of the piece wasn't a Conservative (although some may say he acted like one). Tony Blair built on these reforms by introducing Foundation Trusts and Hospitals in 2003 which gave hospitals more control over their finances and services they provided. The Coalition government transferred all remaining NHS Trusts to Foundation Trusts in 2014.

By the end of 1989, therefore, the NTB had given Thatcherism a new intellectual lease of life. It provided the theoretical arguments to extend individualism within the state sector. Indeed, just as share and home ownership had created 'popular capitalism', the NTB had advocated 'popular individualism' within the state sectors of health and education. Purists, however, would critique the documents and say that they weren't that revolutionary at all: their changes kept everything operating within the state sector. After all, in both their documents, services were still entirely funded by the state, although the NTB did encourage individuals to opt out and supported, and sought to extend, the tax deductibility of private healthcare. However, they rightly noted from a practical point that provision in the private sectors of health and education was too limited. To make the revolution lasting, it needed *popular* support in every definition of the word. Choice and preferences needed to be extended as far as possible which meant operating initially within the state sector. Give individuals a taste of choice and it would ease transition to full denationalisation later, rather than the shock therapy of immediate privatisation. Indeed, so popular were these reforms that, in one way or another, they were not wholly repudiated by successive Labour governments. They were built upon.

V

Europe had never been far away from the fault line of Conservative politics since British entry to the Community in 1973. It had bubbled under the surface since Mrs Thatcher's ascension to the premiership. The early dispute over the British contribution to the EEC budget showed that Mrs Thatcher was not being *Communautaire*. Rather than defending the European interest, she banged the table for 'our money'.

One reason for the Conservatives' embrace of European integration was the 'common' market. It was another means for British export, hundreds of millions more customers for British goods. Conservative MPs saw it as a check on domestic and foreign socialism. The breaking down of trade and regulatory barriers was a very Thatcherite concept. As a result, the government passed the Single European Act in 1986. It sought to Thatcherise the European Community. There was, however, one almighty flaw. For the first time it provided for 'qualified majority' voting at the European Council. The national veto was no longer sacrosanct, meaning a Prime Minister could not block decisions. The second reading of the Bill passed easily, although with notable dissent from 92 Group members Nick Budgen and Teddy Taylor and the NTB's Neil Hamilton (who was also a member of the 92).[28]

The ideological lines on 'Europe' were redrawn by EC Commission President Jacques Delors in a speech to the Trades Union Congress in 1988. From this moment Labour transitioned to be the party of Europe, the

---

[28] As proof of fluid politics both Tony Blair and Gordon Brown voted against the SEA. See Hansard, Commons Debates, 23 April 1986, Vol., Col. 396.

Conservatives (eventually) the sceptics. Delors spoke of creating a social Europe, defending 'social protection', improved working conditions, guaranteed 'social rights', and protections via 'collective agreement' which, to any Thatcherite, protected the closed shop at a European level.[29] Since 1979 the Thatcherite project had put trade union reform at the heart of its agenda. After three careful pieces of legislation and the defeat of the NUM in 1985, the European Community sought to reverse it within the new 'social Europe'. The problem for the Thatcherites was that the EC was now prepared to use the weapons designed for market liberalisation as a mechanism for ever closer political union, harmonisation and state intervention.

Mrs Thatcher hit the roof and replied on 20 September with a carefully worded speech at Bruges which, whilst sticking to a fundamentally pro-European line, kick started the formal Conservative civil war on European integration. The speech is remembered for Mrs Thatcher's explanation that European integration now conflicted with the Thatcherite goal of reducing the size and scope of the state. She said that the UK had not rolled back the frontiers of the state at home only to see them reimposed at a European level from Brussels. She called for a Europe of free enterprise, reduced barriers to trade, wider choice, and less government intervention. All of this meant pluralism, not harmonisation, and was interpreted as a direct challenge to the increasing accumulation of power by the EC, something that Mrs Thatcher had permitted with the passage of the Single European Act.

---

[29] Jacques Delors, '1992: The Social Dimension', speech to the TUC, 8 September 1988,
https://ec.europa.eu/commission/presscorner/api/files/document/print/en/speech_88_66/SPEECH_88_66_EN.pdf

A year later the NTB published a spirited defence of Mrs Thatcher's Bruges Speech in *Europe: Onwards from Bruges*. Her speech, they wrote, was European in tone and content, but wrapped in nuance between 'holier than thou' Europeanism and the nationalism of the nineteenth century.[30] Like Mrs Thatcher they saw the benefits of a common market, not common government, and the Europe they sought was not one that entailed political union or the centralisation of power. Delors wanted eighty per cent of economic decisions being made in Brussels; this had to be resisted.

Their nightmare vision for Europe, and what eventually happened, was the Delors agenda of centralisation, harmonisation and intervention. The alternative, still theoretically within the confines of EC membership, was free trade. This required the EC not to distort the market with subsidies and tariffs. Removing barriers to trade did not mean enforcing common standards. The market and competition would ensure best practice whilst still providing the breathing room for innovation. To the NTB this meant, among others, the phasing out of farming subsidies within fifteen years. It meant a level playing field by the absence of interventionist policies. But this meant dramatically scaling back EC ambitions for statehood, which they weren't going to do. The next step was its boldest: a common currency.

The concept of a single European currency was not new. Edward Heath declared it an ambition when the UK joined the EEC, with a goal for completion by 1980. Since 1972 the EEC had operated a 'snake in the tunnel' economic policy to harmonise exchange rates. Member states agreed to keep their currency values within certain

---

[30] NTB, *Europe: Onwards from Bruges* (London: CPC, 1989), p. 3.

limits of the US dollar. James Callaghan had kept the UK out of the European Monetary System in 1978, which applied more rigid exchange rate harmonisation. In 1988 Delors revived the idea of economic and monetary union. His report in 1989 proposed the creation of a European Central Bank and, with it, a European currency. The abolition of the pound sterling was a step too far, exposed the tensions within Thatcherism and explains how some Thatcherites embraced European integration. They were caught between a classically liberal desire for unfettered freedom and trade, which a fully integrated common market provided, and a conservative's adherence to the nation state and the sovereignty of that state's political institutions, which Europe now threatened.[31] The NTB, however, had a cunning way around this.

The NTB believed that a common currency was just another form of harmonisation. Those fawning over it were just going along with 'fashionable' pro-Europeanism.[32] There was no political will, popular support, or necessity for it. Their alternative, rather, was to allow the new European currency to compete with national currencies across Europe. Individuals could decide themselves which currency to buy, sell, invest, and save in. The 'logic of free trade demands free trade in currencies'.[33] Competing currencies would mean governments would implement more disciplined monetary policies as custom would gravitate to the soundest. This, in turn, would lead to exchange, inflation, and interest rates getting closer together, with competition leading them into stability and, for most EC currencies, reduced inflation and stable interest rates.

---

[31] It arguably had done since 1973.
[32] NTB, *Europe: Onwards from Bruges* (London: CPC, 1989), p. 12.
[33] Ibid., p. 13.

When they were known as the 'Disciples' they didn't specify whether they were following Hayek, Adam Smith or Friedman. We can now answer the question. This was a Hayekian policy. In 1976 Hayek published the *Denationalisation of Money* and argued for a free market in currencies. Writing during a period where British inflation tipped over 25% in the mid-1970s, Hayek argued that states had failed to supply sound money. The alternative was discipline through competition in the market, even allowing for the creation of private currencies. Hayek, therefore, is the godfather of today's cryptocurrencies.

Mrs Thatcher's views hardened considerably against the single currency, and so for that matter did the diehards in the NTB. In 1989 she was ambushed by her Chancellor and Foreign Secretary on the eve of the Madrid EC Summit to support British entry into the European Exchange Rate Mechanism of the European Monetary System. This pegged sterling to the deutschmark and would be the undoing of her successor. Mrs Thatcher refused to give a date for entry, further angering her Chancellor. Lawson resigned later in 1989 over Mrs Thatcher's reliance on Sir Alan Walters as her chief economic adviser. His replacement, John Major, took Britain into the ERM in 1990 and in June proposed that a 'hard ECU' (European Currency Unit) should be formed to compete alongside national currencies.

Had the plans ended there, it would have been another victory for the NTB (via Hayek). The Chancellor and the EC, however, saw the ECU as merely a staging point towards a common European currency. The hard ECU pleased pro-Europeans because it meant Britain was taking a step forward to European Union. It pleased the sovereigntists because it ran alongside the pound and was not an immediate threat to the existence of sterling.

For free marketeers it meant discipline: a hard ECU could hedge against an incoming Labour government (or a Heathite Conservative) turning on the spending taps. Indeed, had the European Community endorsed the idea of an ECU floating alongside national currencies, as the NTB recommended, and ended matters there, it could have avoided the whole Conservative fallout over the single currency and even Brexit itself.

VI

Given its success influencing government policy, especially on education, there had been attempts to rein in the NTB providing a formal manifesto for the 1987 election. 'Wet' and jittery MPs warned Mrs Thatcher that 'the Opposition will point the finger at the more radical proposals and say this is what you really mean to do', and the NTB were dissuaded from issuing a draft manifesto.[34] In 1989, looking at its influence on health and education and with an eye to the next election as early as 1991, the NTB would not be deterred again. Their draft papers included combining existing government departments to 'reduce the overall size of Government'. Energy and Employment would go to Trade and Industry, Social Security to the Treasury, and Fisheries and Food to Health.[35] They sought to appeal to the 'skilled working class' by highlighting policies on law and order and welfare. Being radical on social security was important because 'most of our natural supporters don't think they are ever going to have to rely on it'. On pensions 'more and more are making provision by way of occupational pensions' in order not to turn to the state. Finally, social security reform showed 'that the Government has not "run out of steam" and "still has a job to do"'.[36] Mrs Thatcher encouraged the development of a manifesto at a private dinner at the Institute of Economic Affairs in 1990. She said she was 'disappointed that the group [...] had not yet drawn up its "shopping

---

[34] THCR 6/2/3/35 f136, Stephen Sherborne to Margaret Thatcher, 24 February 1987.
[35] Howarth papers, Angela Rumbold to NTB, circa July 1989.
[36] Howarth papers, Edward Leigh to NTB, circa July 1989.

list" for the next election'.³⁷ As with the first NTB paper, she had prompted another.

The resulting pamphlet was *Choice and Responsibility – The Enabling State,* the NTB's most radical set of proposals for the 'next ten years'. Its opening section demonstrated the effect that Europe already had on Conservative politics. It was less sympathetic to European integration than *Onwards* from *Bruges*. In that document they had not made an issue of sovereignty. The motivating factor was individualism and free markets across Europe, with the market as a check on state power, and even state currencies. But in the space of a year the ground had shifted, especially after the pro-European Sir Anthony Meyer had challenged Mrs Thatcher for the leadership in 1989. The NTB came out swinging.

The fall of the Berlin Wall in 1989 had cemented 'new realities'. Collectivism and socialism were anachronisms, individual freedom and capitalism had triumphed. Even so, the new consensus within the Conservative party that embraced freedom and individualism was still resisted by a 'small but significant element' that believed it could hold socialism at bay with subsidies, cooperation and 'hand outs' delivered by Europe, if not by Westminster.³⁸ Resistance to Thatcherism in the Conservative party was brewing.

There was, however, a bigger debate going on inside the party. Since Mrs Thatcher's Bruges speech, her personal antipathy to the EC had grown, not least after the Madrid 'ambush' over the ERM. In October 1990 she said 'no, no, no' to the suggestion of European political

---

³⁷ Howarth papers, Our chief political correspondent, 'Thatcher to fight election "on radical manifesto"', *The Times*, 22 May 1990.
³⁸ Michael Brown, Gerald Howarth et. al., *Choice and Responsibility – The Enabling State* (London: Conservative Political Centre, 1990), p. 5.

union. The NTB position had hardened as well. They made 'no apology for opening' *Choice and Responsibility* with a defence of 'our nation's sovereignty'. The threats to British sovereignty from a single currency were such that [...] *there can be no equivocation.'*[39] It opposed a single currency and preferred an opt-in Exchange Rate Mechanism without a treaty obligation, one 'we can enter when we can, and should leave when our own interests so demand'. If other nations signed up to the single currency, then the UK should become 'a kind of free port linking Europe and the world'.[40] They still maintained, as they had in *Onwards from Bruges*, that the Single European Act was a force for good by reducing trade barriers. But that was where it should stop as it had achieved its purpose. It was a grim foreboding of the trouble the successor to the Single European Act, the Maastricht Treaty, was to provide.

On privatisation they urged the government to go further by selling off British Coal, the London Underground, British Rail, the Post Office, and air traffic control. They also called for road charging, a very radical policy that has divided libertarians for decades. It is worth acknowledging the power of the document at this point. The Major administration, much decried by Thatcherites for its moderation, privatised British Coal in 1994 and completed British Rail denationalisation by 1997. It also attempted liberalisation of the Post Office in 1994, defeated by a rebellion within the party, and in their 1997 manifesto they pledged to privatise the London Underground. Tony Blair carried on the revolution by part-privatising air traffic control in 2000.

Its final and most radical section came under the title 'The Withering of the State', a play on Marxist

---

[39] Ibid., pp. 7-8. Italics are their emphasis.
[40] Ibid., p. 9.

terminology. Using Maoist phraseology it called for 'a great leap forward' with citizens providing 'themselves with non-emergency health care, education and pensions'.[41] It was a significant 'leap' in their thinking, going beyond widening choice within the public sector. Now they wanted to extend that choice as wide as possible to dramatically reduce the role and size of the state. As choice had been introduced within the state sector through the 1988 education reforms and the NHS internal market, the next logical step for the Thatcherites was to increase supply in the independent sector too. Thus, the NTB now advocated vouchers, with parents allowed to top up if needed. Other state schools would become 'contractual bodies' to the state so they could 'compete on equal terms' with the independent sector.

The document is peak Thatcherism. Further policies included portable pensions, abolition of the forty pence higher rate tax bracket, a reduction of the lower rate to fifteen per cent, state benefits to be converted into 'a private insurance system', and a gradual transfer of mortgage tax relief into 'a single, new investment relief'.[42] Mrs Thatcher is unlikely to have supported this last point, however. She had battled her previous Chancellors over this, such was her 'devotion to the cause of the homebuyer' and mortgage interest relief.[43] Yet in total the document provided an agenda for the fourth term that built on the eleven years that preceded it. The tax cuts, privatisations, the extension of choice, giving power to consumers and not producers in public service provision all set Thatcherism on the path set out in *Choice and Responsibility*. It is ironic that it came at a point when

---

[41] Ibid., p. 18.
[42] Ibid., pp. 19-20.
[43] Nigel Lawson, *The View from No. 11: Memoirs of a Tory Radical* (London: Transworld Publishers Ltd., 1993), p. 11.

Mrs Thatcher's grip on the party was weakening, although as mentioned her successors implemented parts of it.

The media fallout split an already fractious Tory party. The implementation of the Community Charge, a single, flat-rate rate payment for local services that was spiralling out of control, as well as Mrs Thatcher's euroscepticism, was proving deeply unpopular with significant elements in the parliamentary party. Jerry Hayes, the Conservative MP for Harlow, said that, if implemented, *Choice and Responsibility* would prove to be 'an electoral albatross' and lead to 'fratricides of Bennite proportions', Tony Benn having split the Labour party in 1981 with his deputy leadership challenge on a left-wing platform.[44] The 'Tory press' were more welcoming. *The Times* wrote that ministers had 'been parroting the speeches used by Labour and Tory ministers alike since the war', accusing them of going 'public-sector native'. Public spending, the article argued, was running '10 per cent higher in real terms' than when Mrs Thatcher took office. Rather, the government should heed the proposals as 'The New Right still has some of the best tunes in British politics'.[45] The *Daily Telegraph* said that whilst 'there is much [...] with which we cannot agree [...] the group is surely right to demand debate',[46] and the *Daily Mail* said knee-jerk reactions were 'no reason for dismissing the suggestions out of hand'.[47] Even if Mrs Thatcher's stock was falling, Thatcherism was still far from finished.

---

[44] Howarth papers, Alan Travis, 'Thatcher told to disown welfare plans', *Guardian*, 17 September 1990.
[45] Howarth papers, Leader, 'Still the Best Tunes', *The Times*, 17 September 1990.
[46] Howarth papers, Leader, 'Time for Debate', *Daily Telegraph*, 18 September 1990.
[47] Howarth papers, Leader, 'Right foot forward', *Daily Mail*, 17 September 1990.

VII

Within weeks of the publication of *Choice and Responsibility* Mrs Thatcher had been ousted as Prime Minister by her own MPs. By then the Community Charge, which had led to rioting in central London, had brought the government to a low ebb in the polls. Defeats at by-elections emphasised the government's unpopularity and Mrs Thatcher was no longer seen as the vote winner she once was. The resignation of Sir Geoffrey Howe from the government had invited Michael Heseltine's fateful challenge. Politicians, ultimately, give as much thought to their own seats as they do to the ideas motivating their political behaviour.

The leadership crisis of 1990 split the NTB. After Mrs Thatcher had won the first leadership ballot, but not by the margin required, many around her thought she was finished. On the evening of the 21 November, Peter Lilley is reported to have told Mrs Thatcher that the game was up as she met the cabinet one by one to canvass support. Upon hearing the news that she was going to resign, the diehards in the NTB rushed to Downing Street that evening to dissuade her. Neil Hamilton was the last to leave at 2am, although Edward Leigh and Michael Brown attempted a last-minute campaign as dawn broke later that morning.

Although unable to dissuade her, the NTB left a legacy as Mrs Thatcher's intellectual Praetorian Guard. Their pamphlets and ideas boosted the government when it was drifting. They thought carefully about public policy and the impact their views had not only changed the Conservative party, but the policies and ideas of successive governments. They wanted a permanent revolution. They made one.

About the Author

Dr Tim Aker is the Academic Director of the Margaret Thatcher Centre. He has a PhD and MA from the University of Buckingham. Formerly he was a Member of the European Parliament and a borough councillor. He lives with his family in Kent.

THE BRUGES GROUP

The Bruges Group is an independent all-party think tank. Set up in 1989, its founding purpose was to resist the encroachments of the European Union on our democratic self-government. The Bruges Group spearheaded the intellectual battle to win a vote to leave the European Union and against the emergence of a centralised EU state. With personal freedom at its core, its formation was inspired by the speech of Margaret Thatcher in Bruges in September 1988 where the Prime Minister stated, "We have not successfully rolled back the frontiers of the State in Britain only to see them re-imposed at a European level."

We now face a more insidious and profound challenge to our liberties – the rising tide of intolerance. The Bruges Group challenges false and damaging orthodoxies that suppress debate and incite enmity. It will continue to direct Britain's role in the world, act as a voice for the Union, and promote our historic liberty, democracy, transparency, and rights. It spearheads the resistance to attacks on free speech and provides a voice for those who value our freedoms and way of life.

WHO WE ARE

Founder President:
The Rt Hon. The Baroness Thatcher of Kesteven LG, OM, FRS

Former President:
The Rt Hon. The Lord Tebbit CH PC

Vice-President:
The Rt Hon. The Lord Lamont of Lerwick, PC (1993 – 2024)

Chairman:
Barry Legg

Director:
Robert Oulds MA, FRSA

Washington D.C. Representative:
John O'Sullivan CBE

Founder Chairman:
Lord Harris of High Cross

Former Chairmen:
Dr Brian Hindley, Dr Martin Holmes & Professor Kenneth Minogue

Academic Advisory Council:
Professor Tim Congdon
Dr Richard Howarth
Professor Patrick Minford
Andrew Roberts
Martin Howe, KC
John O'Sullivan, CBE

Sponsors and Patrons:
E P Gardner Dryden
Gilling-Smith
Lord Kalms
David Caldow
Andrew Cook
Lord Howard
Brian Kingham
Lord Pearson of Rannoch
Eddie Addison
Ian Butler
Thomas Griffin
Lord Young of Graffham
Michael Fisher
Oliver Marriott
Hon. Sir Rocco Forte
Michael Freeman
Richard E.L. Smith

MEETINGS

The Bruges Group holds regular high–profile public meetings, seminars, debates, and conferences. These enable influential speakers to contribute to the European debate. Speakers are selected purely by the contribution they can make to enhance the debate.

For further information about the Bruges Group, to attend our meetings, or join and receive our publications, please see the membership form at the end of this paper. Alternatively, you can visit our website www.brugesgroup.com or contact us at info@brugesgroup.com.

Contact us
For more information about the Bruges Group please contact:
Robert Oulds, Director
The Bruges Group, 246 Linen Hall, 162-168 Regent Street, London W1B 5TB
Tel: +44 (0)20 7287 4414 Email: info@brugesgroup.com

www.brugesgroup.com